America's First Centennial Celebration

THE MINUTE MAN AT CONCORD

AMERICA'S FIRST CENTENNIAL CELEBRATION

The Nineteenth of April 1875
at Lexington and
Concord, Massachusetts

by DAVID B. LITTLE

Second Edition

HOUGHTON MIFFLIN COMPANY
BOSTON 1974

First Printing H

Library of Congress Cataloging in Publication Data

Little, David B
  America's first centennial celebration.

  1. Lexington, Battle of, 1775-   Anniversaries,
etc. I. Title.
[E241.L6L5 1974]   973.3'311   73-18201
ISBN 0-395-18466-5

Printed in the United States of America

FOREWORD

BICENTENNIAL TIME IS BEARING DOWN ON THE EASTERN SEABOARD, its press releases rumbling like distant thunder over the heads of the apprehensive inhabitants. Lexington and Concord, Massachusetts, will face it first, just as they faced the first Centennial and the first battle of the American Revolution. Conditions were tough for the two towns and their visitors on April 19, 1775, even tougher in 1875. No one likes to think about what may happen in 1975 if that celebration is too well attended.

Of all the important anniversaries, only the original event in 1775 took place in warm and comfortable weather. The Centennial was celebrated under conditions agreeable to a musk ox. Snow and sleet were uninvited guests at the 150th anniversary in 1925. The thought of 50,000 automobiles converging on Lexington and Concord for the Bicentennial is not a happy one, no matter what the weather.

We find it hard to believe today that the President of the United States could move about so freely, without fears for his safety and comfort, as President Grant did in 1875. Nor can I imagine a situation today where an unruly mass of several thousand strangers in a cold and crowded tent could be brought to order by the voice of one man unaided either by police or a public address system. Yet the Presidents of the Day, E. R. Hoar in Concord and Thomas M. Stetson in Lexington, did precisely that, saving the formal portion of the Centennial from disaster and bringing the day to a triumphal close.

The Grand Army of the Republic was in its prime in 1875. Veterans' organizations abounded. There were thousands of men ready and eager to march, plenty of veteran officers to lead them. The troops did well in parades, but while moving in and out of Lexington and Concord, their officers managed to lead some of them astray, just as they had on several occasions during the War Between the States.

America was in an expansionist mood. The war was over; people were moving west; bigger was better; and the sky was the limit. Perhaps a generation sickened by the Vietnam War will not respond to the Bicentennial with the enthusiasm displayed by the post–Civil War generation. We are closer today to the men of 1775 in our questioning of authority, however, than we are to those of 1875. It was not a great military force that began the American Revolution; it was a great ideal: a ruler is fit to be obeyed only so long as the ruler himself obeys the laws laid down by God for the welfare of his people.

I join other more distinguished authors in my debt to Walter Muir Whitehill, retired Director of the Boston Athenaeum, for encouragement and advice in sifting this story from the mass of material available. The staff of the Concord Free Public Library aided me in learning more about the Centennial than anyone else would care to know. My wife saw to it that I followed Walter Whitehill's suggestions. The Club of Odd Volumes did me the honor of publishing the results in a limited edition for its members.

But most of all I am indebted to my grandmother Barrett at whose knee I learned the family version of the Concord Fight. Thanks to her, for the first ten years of my life I thought that my ever-so-great grandfather Colonel James Barrett whipped the British at the Old North Bridge single-handed.

DAVID B. LITTLE

ILLUSTRATIONS

THE MINUTE MAN AT CONCORD   *Frontispiece*
"The thunderbolt falls on an inch of ground; but the light of it fills the horizon." Keith Martin photograph.

EBENEZER HUBBARD   11
His contribution set in motion the erection of the Minute Man statue and the reconstruction of the Old North Bridge to provide access to it. Painted by Wilbur Fiske Noyes from a contemporary photograph. Courtesy of the Concord Free Public Library. Keith Martin photograph.

VIEW OF THE BATTLEGROUND AT CONCORD, MASSACHUSETTS   13
F. H. Lane, del. Printed by Thayer's Lithography, Boston. This is the view that upset Ebenezer Hubbard. Courtesy of the Concord Free Public Library. Edward J. Moore photograph.

ILLUMINATED COPY OF ACT OF CONGRESS, April 22, 1874   15
presenting ten pieces of condemned brass cannon to the town of Concord for use in casting the statue of the Minute Man. Courtesy of the Concord Free Public Library. Edward J. Moore photograph.

THE OLD NORTH BRIDGE, CONCORD, April 19, 1775   17
From an engraving by Amos Doolittle, copied by Sidney Smith. Courtesy of the Concord Free Public Library. Edward J. Moore photograph.

THE OLD NORTH BRIDGE, CONCORD, 1875   18
Embellished with two rustic half-arbors and a paling of graceful pattern made of cedars with the bark on. Watercolor painting by an unknown artist. Courtesy of the Concord Free Public Library. Edward J. Moore photograph.

PRESIDENT GRANT AND PARTY   19
Outside the residence of Judge Hoar in Concord. Identified on the stereopticon view as follows, from left to right: Vice-President Henry Wilson, President Grant, Secretary of War William W. Belknap, Secretary of State Hamilton Fish, Secretary of Navy George M. Robeson, Secretary of Interior Columbus Delano, Postmaster General Marshall Jewell. T. Lewis, Cambridgeport, photograph.

THE NINETEENTH OF APRIL, 1775, IS AN IMPORTANT DATE IN American history. On that day the American colonists fired upon British troops and forced them to retreat to Boston, thus beginning the revolution which gave birth to the United States. Lexington and Concord shared the responsibility for this battle modestly enough until September 2, 1824, when General Lafayette visited Concord. Hearts were full of joy and gratitude during the farewell tour of this beloved revolutionary hero. Oratory rang like peals of great bells across the land.

The Honorable Samuel Hoar at Concord, in a widely reported speech, told the General that he stood upon the very ground where "the first forcible resistance" was raised against the British crown. This statement, so obvious and true to Concord people, shocked Lexington by its incredible presumption and its reckless disregard of the facts.

Lexington extracted depositions from ten surviving witnesses or participants, very different in tenor from those prepared in 1775, to refute Concord's outrageous claim. Concord could produce depositions, too, and did, thus clouding the issue even further. Each town proved to its own satisfaction that it is indeed the Birthplace of American Liberty and there the matter stands today.

In 1870, ninety-five years after the battles on Lexington green and at Concord's Old North Bridge, both towns began to lay plans for the one-hundredth anniversary. Theirs would be the first of a series of centennial celebrations culminating with the anniversary of the adoption of the Declaration of Independence in Philadelphia on July 4, 1876. These first two celebrations would be important enough to warrant the expense of a permanent memorial in each town to be dedicated on the occasion.

These were serious undertakings for two small farming communities. Lexington had 2,277 inhabitants in 418 dwelling houses, according to the Rev. Elias Nason's *Gazetteer of the State of Massachusetts* published in 1876. Concord's families were larger, her 2,413 inhabitants occupying 391 dwellings. Both towns are located northwest of Boston, Lexington ten miles and Concord eighteen miles distant.

Concord, characteristically enough, had to be kicked into action by the death of a stubborn old farmer named Ebenezer Hubbard. He had insisted that the monument built by the town and dedicated in 1836 on the town's two-hundredth birthday stood on the wrong side of the Concord river. It was indeed on the spot where the British had been during the battle at the Old North Bridge because the west, or American, bank was no longer accessible except through the pasture land of Stedman Buttrick. The western shore was low and swampy, causing grave inconvenience to travelers on the frequent occasions when the river rose over its banks and flooded the road. The town moved the bridge several hundred yards downstream, therefore, in 1793, straightening the road and relocating its western part on higher ground. This action left the east bank within easy reach of the new road and made it the obvious if not the sentimental spot for a monument.

Mr. Hubbard felt strongly enough about the location of the monument to give $600.00 to the town treasurer towards the cost of a new bridge on the site of the old. If the bridge were rebuilt, he reasoned, the town might be more

EBENEZER HUBBARD

interested in erecting a monument on the west bank. The town treasurer accepted his money but the town took no action.

Ebenezer Hubbard lived alone in the old house where his grandfather had entertained John Hancock and the members of the Provincial Congress when it met in the meeting house nearby. He died alone, too, at the vast old age of eighty-seven and his neighbors found him sitting dead in his chair one October morning in 1870.

Death did not stop his mission, however. It brought it to a successful fulfillment far beyond his wildest dreams. Although Ebenezer Hubbard is forgotten today, his contribution set in motion the erection of the Minute Man statue and the reconstruction of the Old North Bridge to provide access to it. These were the central features of Concord's Centennial Celebration. They have made Concord a magnet ever since to all who respect and love human freedom.

"I order my Executor," he wrote in his will, "to pay the sum of one thousand dollars towards building a monument in said town of Concord on the spot where the Americans fell, on the opposite side of the river from the present Monument, in the battle of the Nineteenth of April, 1775, providing my said Executor shall ascertain that said Monument first named has been built, or sufficient funds have been obtained therefor within five years after my decease; but in case my Executor shall have ascertained that said first named Monument is not built, nor sufficient funds obtained for that purpose within five years after my decease, then I order my Executor to pay over to Hancock, N. H., said sum of one thousand dollars."

What had seemed ridiculous for so long now became a brilliant idea. The Concord town meeting in March 1872 appointed a committee to study it and to make a recommendation at the next town meeting in 1873. Town affairs move slowly. Stedman Buttrick expressed his support of the proposal by deeding to the town a quarter of an acre of land on the west side of the

VIEW OF THE BATTLEGROUND AT CONCORD, MASSACHUSETTS

Concord river at the abutment of the Old North Bridge "for the purpose of erecting a Monument thereon and for no other purpose, and on condition that the grantee shall make and forever maintain a fence around the same, and that a bridge shall be constructed across the river from the easterly side to pass to the above premises, and without any right of way over my land."

The committee presented its report in 1873, recommending that the bequest of Ebenezer Hubbard and the gift of Stedman Buttrick be accepted, that a statue of a Continental minute man be cut in granite and erected on a proper foundation on the American side of the river, that a suitable footbridge be constructed to give access to the spot and that the work be completed and dedicated on the hundredth anniversary of the day, with such other exercises as may be hereafter determined. All agreed that the first verse of Emerson's "Concord Hymn" should be carved on the pedestal.

"To do this worthily," said the chairman of the committee John S. Keyes, "let us avail ourselves of these bequests in the patriotic spirit that inspired the givers, and fully understand that if we, as a community, desire ever to do anything to make our battle-ground more memorable this is the fittest occasion."

After due deliberation the committee chose a young, unknown and untried Concord sculptor, Daniel C. French, to make the statue, basing their decision on their admiration for a small plaster model of a minute man which he had submitted to them. On his recommendation the material of the statue was changed from granite to bronze.

The General Court passed an act on March 9, 1874, authorizing the Town of Concord to raise money for a monument and for its dedication. At the town meeting the next week Concord voted to raise $1,500.00 for this purpose and also appointed a Centennial Committee to prepare for a suitable celebration.

The Honorable Ebenezer Rockwood Hoar, a distinguished Concord citizen, grandson of the Samuel who was Lafayette's host in 1824, Grant's Attorney-General from 1869 to 1870 and a member of the House of Representatives, 43rd Congress, persuaded the Congress to give to the town ten pieces of condemned brass cannon to be used in casting the statue. The act passed the house on April 18, the Senate on April 20, and was approved by President Grant on April 22. Soon thereafter the cannon were sent to the Ames Manufacturing Company in Chicopee, Massachusetts.

Daniel French completed the full-size plaster model early in the autumn and shipped it to the foundry to be cast.

The appearance of the Old North Bridge was well known through the

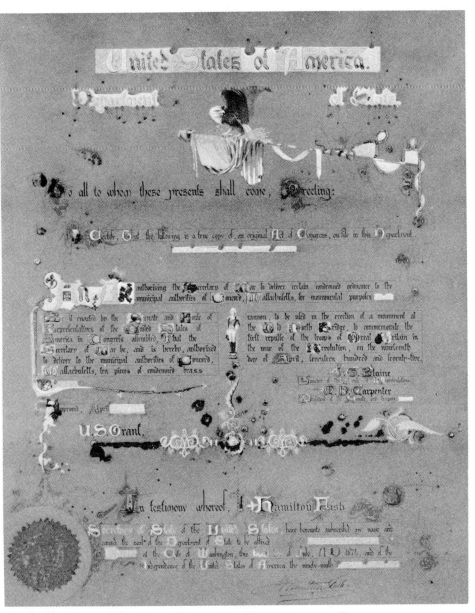

ILLUMINATED COPY OF ACT OF CONGRESS, APRIL 22, 1874

medium of the 1775 engraving by Amos Doolittle. The committee intended to make the new bridge resemble the old one but, appalled by its simplicity, they substituted for the railing of the original a confection described as "a paling of graceful pattern made of cedars with the bark on." They also added two rustic half-arbors on the middle projecting over the water and containing seats for the weary.

Mindful of the tendency of the west bank to disappear under water, the committee brought in fill and built up the land given by Mr. Buttrick to the level of the old abutment. They planted a willow hedge around its margin to hold with its roots this new hillock against the insidious fingers of spring floods.

Lexington, blessed with the presence of her devoted and beloved historian Charles Hudson, had a plan for a permanent memorial derived from the efforts of the Lexington Monument Association during the years after its incorporation in 1850. The War Between the States had brought its work to a standstill but not its hopes. Soon after the war the Association succeeded in building a Memorial Hall and placing in it marble statues of a minute man and a Union soldier. Two more niches were prepared and left vacant for statues of John Hancock and Samuel Adams. Both gentlemen had been in Lexington on the morning of the battle.

Early in 1873, therefore, the Lexington committee commissioned two American sculptors resident in Italy, Thomas R. Gould of Florence and Martin Milmore of Rome, to carve these statues from Carrara marble and to deliver them in Lexington not later than January 1, 1875.

The Lexington committee wrote a letter to Concord's Board of Selectmen on November 12, 1873, inviting Concord to join with Lexington in the Centennial Celebration as Lexington had joined with Concord on the Seventy-Fifth. Concord declined the opportunity for a joint observance by vote of the town meeting in March 1874.

THE OLD NORTH BRIDGE, CONCORD, APRIL 19, 1775

The rivalry between the two towns rose to a fever pitch as the Centennial approached, not among their leaders, who were working together as closely as intelligent men sometimes can, but among the ordinary citizens. Lexington expressed considerable satisfaction that she would dedicate two statues to Concord's one, statues carved in Italy by distinguished sculptors. Who had ever heard of Daniel C. French?

THE OLD NORTH BRIDGE, CONCORD, 1875

January 1, 1875, came and passed without the promised arrival of the statues. Frantic letters were exchanged across the Atlantic at the leisurely pace of the day, finally bringing the glad tidings that the statues had been shipped.

Concord cut the pedestal for its Minute Man from the same great boulder of Westford granite that had provided the stone for the monument dedicated in 1836 on the opposite shore. The committee installed it in March on the center line of the bridge, 110 feet from the western end, just in front of the old sprouting apple stump where, according to tradition, Isaac Davis fell. The statue was placed upon it during the first week in April, admired by

PRESIDENT GRANT AND PARTY

the townspeople for a few days and then veiled to await the ceremonies on the Nineteenth. If Concord felt any sympathy for Lexington at this time, it was not visible.

The April weather was a source of grave concern. Spring had not yet made its appearance and the season was both wet and cold. The Concord river rose above its banks, drowning the low meadow connecting the knoll on which the Minute Man stands and the high land beyond. This was serious as the parade route was now cut between its climax at the unveiling of the statue and its conclusion at the oration tent 100 yards away.

If Concord was in trouble because her statue could be reached only from the new North Bridge, Lexington was in a truly calamitous state with no statues at all. One steamer from Liverpool arrived in Boston, but she had no statue on board and none was listed on her cargo manifest. One more steamer, the *Parthia*, was expected in Boston before the Nineteenth. Lexington crossed her fingers and prayed.

On Saturday morning, April 17, her prayers were answered. The brig *J. L. Bowen* from Leghorn, bearing the statue of John Hancock, was reported weatherbound in Vineyard Haven. The U. S. Revenue Cutter *Gallatin*, Captain Seldon, rushed to her aid and soon had her under tow for Boston. The *Parthia*, Samuel Adams in her hold, docked in East Boston during the forenoon. As soon as possible the statue was loaded on a six-horse team and started for Lexington. It arrived just before midnight.

The *Bowen* docked in Boston Saturday night. Her precious cargo reached Lexington Sunday noon. By sunset on the eve of the Centennial both statues were in place in the pavilion on Lexington green. Twelve hours leeway on a two-year job was close figuring, too close for comfort but time enough for the success of the Centennial.

Residents of Concord and Lexington were not the only ones who were preparing for this affair. The Boston daily newspapers printed the Centennial

WRIGHT'S TAVERN, CONCORD

VIEW OF THE PROCESSION, MONUMENT SQUARE, CONCORD

VIEW OF THE PROCESSION, MONUMENT SQUARE, CONCORD

Celebration programs in full during the week beginning April 12. This was the big news, pushing the Beecher trial and the strike in the Lowell textile mills into the background.

The railroads serving Concord and Lexington had also made their plans. The Framingham and Lowell Railroad published Concord's whole schedule of events on Saturday, April 17, in *The Railroad Advertiser*, a weekly paper circulated free to passengers bound to Lowell, Nashua and the north. Three extra trains were announced from Lowell, Mansfield and South Framingham to Concord Junction in the morning and returning in the evening.

The *Boston Sunday Herald* printed the schedules of the Fitchburg and Lowell railroads for Monday, showing trains running to Concord and Lexington during the morning and back to Boston in the afternoon and evening at half-hour intervals.

THE CELEBRATION IN CONCORD

Preparations moved more rapidly during the final week although the weather remained unsympathetic. Three inches of snow fell during April 13, the day before Concord's dinner tent was to be erected. The road department cleared the tent site and a warm sun dried the ground, enabling the tent to be raised on schedule.

Two tents were erected on George Keyes's meadow within sight of the Minute Man and on the same side of the river. The oration tent occupied the spot on which the Provincial troops made their final formation and from which they attacked the British Light Infantry at the bridge. The tent measured 200 by 85 feet and was capable of holding 6,000 people. A few seats were placed in front near the platform for the ladies. The rest of the audience was expected to stand. The platform stood about two feet above the ground and held seats for 200.

The dinner tent nearby was even larger. Of new snowy canvas 410 feet

THE CONCORD BRIDGE WHICH DAVIS WHEN HE
FOUND WAS THE BEE-LINE TRACK TO HEAVEN AND FAME

ENTRANCE TO THE BATTLEGROUND, CONCORD

long, 85 feet wide, and 40 feet high, crowned with flags, it was viewed with mingled pride and apprehension during the few days preceding the Nineteenth. The interior was profusely decorated with flags, bunting and streamers. Each of the thirteen tent poles displayed a shield bearing the emblem of one of the thirteen original states. Beneath each shield two American flags were gracefully looped. Appropriate mottoes adorned the sides of the canvas.

A platform, table high and twelve feet wide, extended eighty feet across the center of the tent, dividing it into two equal halves. Sixty tables, each seating seventy persons, were placed in rows parallel to the platform and on both sides of it. Tables for the 200 distinguished guests filled the platform.

Located between wind and water on the historic spot from which the first deliberate attack on British troops was launched, the tents were sheltered by the hillside behind them against a strong and gusty north wind which several times threatened their destruction. All of the great skill of their owners, R. M. Yale and Andrew Erickson of Boston, was required to save them on several occasions by partially lowering them during the most severe blasts.

Concord's road department worked steadily to fill and grade sidewalks and roads along the route to make walking comfortable for the expected crowds. All trace of the recent storms had soaked into the ground leaving the surface reasonably dry.

The Concord river reluctantly receded from the meadow into its banks, clearing the way for the procession to pass dry-shod from the Minute Man to the tents beyond.

Concord's Centennial Committee entered the final weekend in a cheerful mood. Saturday morning was encouraging. A warm sun competing with a fresh cold wind looked down on Concord's citizens while they decorated their houses and their town. As the celebration was to be honored by the participation of the President of the United States, the Navy Yards at Portsmouth, Boston, New York and Washington had sent vast quantities of flags and uncut bunting to be displayed on public buildings. Lieut. Comdr. Henry H. Gorringe, U. S. Navy, came to Concord by order of the Secretary of the Navy to take charge of this government material and earned high praise from the committee for his efficient and tactful performance.

The Agricultural Hall, the two tents, public buildings, liberty pole and principal streets were decorated by the town with this borrowed material, while private houses along the route burst into bunting under the hands of their owners.

The committee expected 20,000 visitors on the Nineteenth and had made careful plans to handle them in an orderly manner.

Early in the preliminary discussions the committee had asked Major General Francis C. Barlow of New York to act as Chief Marshal and had appointed thirteen Assistant Marshals to serve as mounted aides in forming and conducting the procession. Five of these Assistant Marshals, all with Boston addresses, were designated to receive from their units a statement of their numbers, their estimated time of arrival in Concord and their means of transportation.

In addition to these Assistant Marshals, representatives were appointed in the various towns invited to share in the celebration to represent the Chief Marshal in their towns and to lead their general delegations in the Fifth Division of the procession. The official delegations from each town were assigned to the Fourth Division.

Mustering points for each division were well publicized and were also marked with banners at each location. All persons intending to join in the procession were asked to familiarize themselves with the position of the division to which they belonged and with their own places in it.

Having done their best to insure the orderly formation of the parade, Concord's committee turned its attention to the control of the spectators. Concord's police force was competent to handle tramps and the other minor diversions from law and order which occur in small towns but no one expected it to cope with a Centennial.

After due negotiations the City of Boston agreed to send Sergeant John H. Laskey of Station 2 with sixty men on Sunday morning to remain in Concord until Tuesday. Details from Worcester, Springfield, Lowell, Fitchburg, Lynn and Salem were also ordered to Concord and placed under Sergeant Laskey's command.

Boston also sent a large force of detectives on the Nineteenth with instructions to mingle with the crowds as a deterrent to the pickpockets who always graced large gatherings with their presence.

In January the committee had written a notice of the Centennial which was printed in most of the New York and New England newspapers and sent by mail in all directions. This was intended to inform the descendents of Concord people, scattered though they were all over the country, that they would be especially welcome on this anniversary day.

This invitation had its desired effect. By Saturday night friends and relations filled the private houses and public accommodations to the bursting point.

First of the official guests to arrive was the Governor of Vermont, the Honorable Asahel Peck, and his escort, the Ransom Guards of St. Albans. Showing traditional Vermont foresight the Guards took no chances on accommodations. They lived comfortably on board their special train through the celebration and returned home as planned on Tuesday morning.

President Grant and his party arrived in Concord at 9:30 Saturday evening and were received at the railroad station by a small group of about 100 persons. Cabinet Secretaries Belknap, Robeson and Delano accompanied the President together with Speaker and Mrs. James G. Blaine of the House. After descending from their palace car the party took carriages to the residence of their host, Judge E. R. Hoar, on Main street.

THE OLD NORTH BRIDGE AND THE MINUTE MAN, 1875

Concord bore the honor of the President's company with a calm border-ing on indifference. He had been invited. He came. A parade by the Concord Artillery, the Ransom Guards and their respective bands provided far better entertainment on this moonlit evening.

Sunday was a miserable day, cold and cheerless with a raw wind which pierced the very marrow of the bones. First excitement of the day was the arrival early in the morning of the Portland Mechanic Blues, escorting the Hon. Nelson Dingley, Jr., Governor of Maine, and his staff.

All three military units in town marched to services at the First Parish meeting house in the morning and at the Congregational Trinitarian Church in the afternoon. President Grant was among the worshippers at the old meeting house in the morning where he heard the Reverend Grindall Reyn-olds preach on the overlapping in the Puritan mind of true religion and true politics, a religious interpretation of the foundation of government which had enabled the colonists to defy the king with a clear conscience. No empty seats could be found in either church at any service. The square outside the old meeting house was packed during the morning with visitors who had tried unsuccessfully to enter.

All this was a novelty to a reporter from the *New York Herald* who wrote, "As provincial New England could do nothing without preaching a sermon over it, or before it, or after it, so republican New England found it impossible to celebrate the past without a reasonable amount of preaching." The Boston newspapers, publishing the texts of some of the sermons for the edification of their readers, saw nothing unusual.

Despite the weather an estimated 2,500 visitors on foot and in carriages had a preview of the celebration, examining the clearly labeled points of in-terest and admiring the decorations. Military uniforms and the gay bunting whipping in the wind provided the only cheerful notes under a leaden sky.

Many who were unable or unwilling to go to church sought consolation at the Middlesex Hotel bar, which did a brisk business until late Sunday afternoon when it was closed by order of the Selectmen. Quiet descended on Concord with the dusk, broken only by the late arrival of visitors, most of whom could find no beds. Stable yards, too, were filled beyond their capacity. Men and beasts passed an uncomfortable night.

The weather report for Monday, April 19, called for generally clear and cold weather with NW to SW winds and slowly rising barometer.

Two cannon from Battery A, First Artillery, M. V. M., under the command of Captain E. C. Langley, left Boston at eleven o'clock Sunday night and rumbled through the streets of Concord before daybreak for their firing position on Nashawtuc Hill. At precisely eighteen minutes past five o'clock the first cannon spoke. One hundred rounds in regular cadence boomed over the town, inaugurating the first Centennial celebration to be held in the United States. The rolling of drums soon joined in the heavy rhythm of the guns, underscoring the clear notes of bugles sounding reveille.

The day had come. Concord's sleepers rose from their beds, if they were lucky enough to have them, and looked out on a cloudless day. The temperature at six o'clock was a cold 22° Fahrenheit. The streets were dry.

The first train from Boston arrived at 7:30 a.m. The Concord reception committee, with headquarters in a tent near the Fitchburg station, swung smoothly into operation. Important guests were conducted to the home of Judge Hoar or to the old court house for breakfast. Veteran military organizations were marched to the Agricultural Hall nearby for the same.

The arrival of more trains at the Fitchburg and the Lowell stations soon swamped the best efforts of the reception committee. No one had imagined that the popular response to this celebration would be so great. The carrying capacity of the roads and railroads set a limit to the number of visitors as many more tried to come than succeeded.

The various organizations assigned to the five divisions marched and countermarched until nine o'clock when they took their assigned places in the formation. Some units, caught in traffic, were late in arriving, further complicating the work of the marshals.

The police had hard work persuading spectators along the line of march to stand clear. Fences, porches, windows and even a few roof tops were crowded. Monument Square, being a large open area, was particularly hard to control, as people in back exerted a constant forward pressure toward a better view and those in front did their best to hold their ground.

The Governor of Massachusetts, the Hon. William Gaston, and his staff arrived at 9:30 under escort of the First Corps of Cadets. He was greeted by a fifteen-gun salute.

A few minutes before ten o'clock twenty-one guns were fired to announce that President Grant and his Cabinet were taking their places in line.

Promptly at ten o'clock Chief Marshal Barlow gave the order to march. The procession moved swiftly down Main street through Monument Square and Monument street toward the bridge.

President Grant, Vice-President Wilson, the Hon. Hamilton Fish, Secretary of State, and General Babcock, Military Secretary to the President, rode in a barouche drawn by four bay horses in the Second Division behind the U. S. Marine Band and the Concord Artillery. The President drew polite cheers from the crowds but their greatest enthusiasm was bestowed upon Major General A. E. Burnside, who marched on foot in the Third Division with the First Light Infantry Veterans Association of Rhode Island. His progress along the route was one continuous ovation.

When the Fifth Regiment, Massachusetts Volunteer Militia, leading the First Division, swung off Monument street into the monument grounds it marched to the right, stopped, faced left and saluted the column as it went by. The British flag hanging at half-mast over the graves of the two British soldiers killed at the bridge provided a mute reminder that wars are lost as well as

THE DINNER TENT, CONCORD

won. Here England lost the first two men among the thousands who "—came three thousand miles and died, to keep the past upon its throne."

The remainder of the First Division crossed the bridge, passed the shrouded figure of the Minute Man and entered the oration tent. As the President's carriage approached, John S. Keyes, Chairman of the Monument Committee, stepped forward and unveiled the statue. A cannon boomed, the crowd cheered and the procession flowed on.

By eleven o'clock the tent had reached about 4,000 of its 6,000 capacity. Most of the first four divisions and a small group admitted before the arrival of the procession were inside. Although the Fifth Division had only reached Monument Square, the President of the Day, the Hon. Ebenezer Rockwood Hoar, called the assemblage to order.

"Friends and fellow citizens, In this solemn hour, when the nation enters upon its second century, on the spot which was its birthplace, let us reverently ask God to be with us, as he was with our fathers."

The Reverend Grindall Reynolds, Chaplain of the Day, then offered a brief and eloquent prayer. He was interrupted in full course by the squeal of tortured timbers and other breaking-up noises. The platform, lacking the stability of the nation, collapsed under the weight of dignity and deposited the President on the ground. In the midst of the resultant confusion a loud clear voice was heard to say, "This evidently is not a third-term platform." Despite the applause which followed this remark, the President maintained a monumental dignity throughout. Judge Hoar soon succeeded in restoring order. The Reverend Grindall Reynolds completed his prayer.

Ralph Waldo Emerson was the next speaker, his subject the statue and the minute man for whom it stands.

"We have no need to magnify the facts," he said. "Only two of our men were killed at the bridge, and four others wounded. But here the British army was first fronted, and driven back; and if only two men, or only one man, had been slain, it was the first victory. The thunderbolt falls on an inch of ground; but the light of it fills the horizon."

Mr. Emerson was seventy-two years old. Although his speech was frequently applauded, his voice was very low and could be heard only by those standing close to the platform. He emphasized almost every sentence by a quaint little bob of his head and spoke with great deliberation. The crowd in the tent became restive and noisy, drowning out the sound of his voice entirely. Judge Hoar then arose and said in a mighty voice audible to all, "Fellow citizens, the sovereign people of America are gentlemen, and when they assemble on a public occasion like this, they will keep order and preserve silence!"

Thunderous applause was followed by absolute silence inside the tent. Outside a band marched past playing "Mulligan's Guards." Distant cheers and catcalls were faintly heard. Mr. Emerson completed his address.

Next on the program was an ode by James Russell Lowell which was not printed in the otherwise complete reporting of the event by Boston and New York papers. Mr. Lowell wanted his ode to appear first in the *Atlantic Monthly* and it did.

During its reading the platform, which had been hastily repaired, collapsed again, causing a momentary disorder and providing the newspaper reporters present with an opportunity for witticisms.

George William Curtis, once of Concord and then of New York, gave the principal address of the day: "The last living links with the Revolution have long been broken. Great events and a mightier struggle have absorbed our own generation. Yet we who stand here today have a sympathy with the men at the Old North Bridge, which those who preceded us here at earlier celebrations could not know."

At ten minutes before one o'clock, before the close of the oration, Mr. Curtis paused at the request of Judge Hoar, who said, "Ladies and gentlemen, Concord always keeps faith with Lexington. We promised to deliver to them the President at one o'clock; and he is therefore obliged to leave. Give him three parting cheers."

The cheers were given with a will. The President, Vice-President, members of the Cabinet, Governor Chamberlain of South Carolina, Governor Gaston, the Executive Council and Legislature of Massachusetts, the Judges of the Supreme Judicial Court and several other important guests who had accepted the Lexington invitation then left the oration tent where events were proceeding close to schedule and soon found themselves lost in a strangely transformed Concord where all forms of communication had vanished. Their adventures and hardships will be told in another place.

Mr. Curtis completed his address. The invited guests passed between two lines of the Fifth Regiment, M. V. M., from the platform entrance of the oration tent to the east door of the dinner tent and took their places at table. The grand entrance on the west end of the dinner tent was then opened to ticket holders from the general public.

Places for 4,000 had been set on Saturday and the cold food set forth could be better described as frozen. To a thoroughly chilled group of diners the dinner had little attraction. Dinner was over in half an hour.

For the next three hours Judge Hoar held the half-frozen audience by the warmth of his personality, aided by the graceful and appropriate remarks of distinguished guests as they responded to the sentiments of the day. Altogether it was an extraordinary performance.

Outside the wind was picking up. Iron-grey clouds swept over the town at a low level, leaving behind them a dusting of snow. Drums, bugles and bands raised a din for the dual purpose of entertaining the thousands for whom there was no room in the tent and of keeping the players from freezing to death.

"I offer as the first regular sentiment of the day," said Judge Hoar, "The

Nineteenth of April, Seventeen Hundred and Seventy-five: A glorious day for Lexington and Concord, for the towns of Middlesex, for Massachusetts, for America, for freedom, and the rights of mankind. 'Every blow struck for liberty among men since the 19th of April 1775, has but echoed the guns of that eventful morning.' "

"First of those who fell, in our memory of the day we celebrate," continued Judge Hoar, "are the martyrs on Lexington Common. Their deeds, their immortal fame, are now being worthily celebrated by their neighbors and descendants at Lexington. I give you:—
The martyrs on Lexington Common,—Parker, Monroe, Hadley, the Harringtons, Muzzey, Brown.

> 'With us their names shall live
> Through long succeeding years,
> Embalmed with all our hearts can give,
> Our praises, and our tears.'

Fellow Citizens, no one from Lexington can be found here today to respond to this sentiment, as I suppose no one from Concord could be found at Lexington to acknowledge any courtesies extended to us. So be it. The legacy of glory will go round, and is enough for all. But I thought it fitting to send, and have sent, in your name, a message to Lexington from Concord, to this effect:—
'Concord sends greetings to Lexington on the hundredth anniversary of the glorious morning, by the hands of the President of the United States. The Great Republic, whose thirty-seven states span the continent from ocean to ocean, is the harvest of which the seed was sown on the 19th of April, 1775.'

"And next in memory," said the Judge, "are the men who were first to fall at the North Bridge at Concord,—Captain Isaac Davis, and Abner Hosmer, a private of his company of Minute Men of Acton, the first to lay down their lives in an organized military attack upon the soldiers of Great Britain in the Revolutionary War. The grateful country for whose liberties they died accords to them a foremost place upon her roll of honor."

The Reverend Franklin P. Wood, pastor of the Centre Congregational Church in Acton, replied gracefully, praising the part played by Captain Davis without minimizing the role of the others at the bridge. Times had changed since the Centennial of the Town of Acton in 1835 when the Hon. Josiah Adams's remarks on the subject stirred up a tremendous row.

"The truth is, it was said so at the time, and ever since," claimed Mr. Adams, "that, when Captain Davis arrived on the ground no one would agree to go in front. When he arrived they took courage. His spirit was known and they relied on it. And I repeat, that the soul of the action on that morning was the soul of Isaac Davis; and when that soul fled the action was over."

Deacon Hayward's response to an unexpected call at Concord's celebration in 1850 was equally blunt. "The Day we Celebrate," he said. "The 19th of April 1775; that day made so glorious in our country's history by the bravery of our people; that day when Concord found the *ground* and Acton the *men!*"

The *New York Herald* reprinted Deacon Hayward's remarks in their issue of April 19, 1875, but if they expected to stir up another row, they were disappointed.

The American Band of Providence played appropriate music between each set of sentiments and responses until finally the increasing cold forced the ceremonies to close with a final sentiment expressed by a citizen of Concord.

"The Tree of Liberty: May it take deep root, and grow until its branches shall cover the whole earth."

It was now nearly five o'clock. The distinguished guests returned to warm firesides to prepare themselves for the delights of the Grand Ball in the evening. The military units also had their havens of refuge. The general public was left to fend for itself.

HALL OF THE MIDDLESEX AGRICULTURAL SOCIETY, CONCORD

And what of the 50,000 or more who had been fending for themselves all day, unable to see or hear any part of the celebration other than the parade in the morning? Their presence in such numbers had not been planned for or expected.

Many wandered over the Hill Burying Ground where Col. James Barrett, Major John Buttrick and a dozen other minute men were buried, their graves marked on this occasion with small American flags. Inscriptions on old tombstones make entertaining reading but not for long on a day so cold that those people above ground are only a little warmer than those below.

Other points of historic interest in the town also had more visitors during this single day than they had had in all the years since they became historic.

The search for food became intense. The Middlesex Hotel in desperation closed its doors to all except those who could produce "Boarder's Tickets" and called in the police to enforce this restriction. A hungry crowd stormed the hotel pantry, gained it briefly, and was thrown out again by the hardworking police.

Other restaurants were swept bare by two o'clock; improvised eating houses, an hour earlier. Fruit, peanut, bread and pie wagons did a splendid business at high prices until their supplies, too, were exhausted.

The Selectmen had one firm idea about handling crowds. They closed the bar again at the Middlesex Hotel late in the afternoon, forcing seekers after liquid cheer to patronize the bootleggers whose bottle business in the streets was booming. Liquor on empty stomachs had the usual effect. The strains of "Saw My Leg Off—Quick!" and other Civil War ballads rose with the fumes of alcohol on Concord streets. Despite the drinking there was very little disorder.

The liveliest scrimmage of the day occurred at the Middlesex Hotel when a gentleman who had taken more than adequate precautions against the cold drove his horse into the stable yard and demanded the service for which the hotel was famous during normal times. The proprietor, exhausted by the crush of patronage during the past few days, asked him to take his business elsewhere. Harsh words were followed by blows, by the police, and by the crowd. The would-be customer fled on foot across Monument Square pursued by the police, who finally collared him despite the interference of the crowd and locked him up. What happened to his horse and rig is not recorded.

By six o'clock most of the crowd had gone home. They were fortunate to be able to do so. The two-track Fitchburg Railroad succeeded in removing at least as many persons in the evening as it had deposited in town in the morning, while the Lowell Railroad, as will be related, was a mess. Almost nothing moved on its single track between Boston and Concord. Lexington, in the middle of the line, was a shambles.

Most of the sixty-eight reporters logged in by the Concord press committee in the morning had departed also. Over a single telegraph line they had filed vast amounts of copy which their editors were sorting out into a vivid and reasonably accurate account of the day for the Tuesday editions. They also left a fervent request to the next Centennial press committee to put practical journalists in charge of press arrangements at that time. There is no substitute, they said, for experience.

Concord's Centennial Committee had wisely chosen to hold their grand ball not in a tent but in the spacious hall of the Middlesex Agricultural Society on the bank of the Sudbury river west of the Fitchburg railroad station. This building had an upper and a lower hall together with several smaller rooms. It was heated throughout and brilliantly lighted by gas. An arch inscribed "1775, April 19th, 1875" adorned the entrance. Festoons of bunting, flags of all nations and shields on either side of the arch increased the festive appearance and gave promise of the even more splendid decorations displayed within. Messrs. Lamprell & Marble of Boston, aided by the tireless Lieut. Comdr. Gorringe, U. S. Navy, left no inch of the hall undecorated.

The ceiling was completely hidden by large flags, the walls by festoons of flags, naval signals and bunting. Trophies of sabre blades arranged in the form of stars on a blue ground gleamed like polished silver in the gaslight. The entire lower floor was cleared and covered with white canvas for the dancers.

Platforms for the musicians stood at both the eastern and western ends of the hall. On the western wall a globe rested on the shield of the United States. Above it an eagle held in its beak a wreath of laurel and olive. On each side hung American flags and sunbursts of muskets on a blue ground spangled with stars. Below it a fragrant bank of potted flowers covered the face of the musicians' platform.

The Grand Orchestra played from this platform under the direction of D. W. Reeves of Providence. The United States Marine Band, resplendent in their dress uniforms, played from the other, starting off at eight o'clock and playing a promenade concert alternately with the Grand Orchestra until the ball began at ten thirty.

About 300 couples danced through the night. Many of the ladies wore colonial costumes, adding the elegance of another age in rich, soft colors to the blinding brilliance of the hall.

From half past eleven until one o'clock William Tufts of Boston served supper in the big upper room. Word reached Concord shortly after midnight that President Grant would not return. Concord had taken his presence calmly during the beginning of the Centennial and showed no grief over his absence at the end.

The sun was rising as the last of the dancers headed for their homes just twenty-four hours after the thudding of cannon had saluted the beginning of the Centennial.

THE CELEBRATION IN LEXINGTON

In Lexington during the week before the Nineteenth preparations followed the same pattern as they had in Concord. Houses were decorated, historic spots marked and two great tents were erected on the old battleground in the center of the village.

A large triumphal arch inscribed "Welcome to the Birthplace of American Liberty" spanned the entrance to the common. Above it an American flag thirty feet long flew from a high pole flanked on each side by a line of smaller flags extending across the two streets.

The two tents occupied a large portion of the common. The pavilion, nearest the arch, was reached from it by an evergreen-bowered path. The dining tent stood close by and was connected to the pavilion by a short covered passage.

The speeches in the morning and the ball in the evening would be held in the pavilion tent. Measuring 200 feet by 80 and intended to hold about 7,000 persons, it was as much of a tourist attraction on Sunday as any of the historic spots in town. Like Concord's oration tent it stood on the spot occupied by the minute men at their time of decision a hundred years before.

The platform for speakers and distinguished guests filled the western end of the tent, its leading edge decorated with green cloth fringed with gold. Trophies of the Revolution, including a flag with red and white stripes and twelve stars flown by the *Bon Homme Richard* during her engagement with the *Serapis*, hung over the speaker's desk in the center. By Sunday night the long-awaited statues of Samuel Adams and John Hancock stood veiled at the right and left ends of the platform with a palmetto tree sent from South Carolina and a Massachusetts pine tree midway between them and the lectern. These trees were symbols of the union between the two states which had been sadly interrupted by the War Between the States.

The dining tent extended the full length of the common, parallel to Elm street, and continued across Bedford street for a total length of 410 feet on an axis roughly at right angles to that of the pavilion. This tent was 50 feet wide and had a wing on one side 100 feet by 50. Its hundred tables were intended to seat about 3,500 guests. Both tents were illuminated by gas, had wooden floors and were lavishly decorated by Colonel William Beals & Sons, the firm responsible for the decoration of the town.

The prices of accommodations in Lexington mounted steadily as the supply decreased, causing anguish both to those who had let their rooms too soon and to those who had applied for rooms too late. Booths and makeshift restaurants sprouted all over town, their proprietors, equipment and supplies arriving by train and wagon in a steady stream. Local merchants were not worried. Amidst the patriotic enthusiasm for the day shone the national instinct for gain.

Idealism was not lacking, however. In addition to the countless hours of work voluntarily and cheerfully accomplished by the Lexington Centennial committees and other local residents, citizens of neighboring towns were generous with their aid. Conspicuous among them were twenty-five young ladies of Cambridge, soon joined by more young ladies from Arlington, who offered to wait on table in the dining tent. The caterer, Mr. J. B. Smith, accepted their offer with gratitude and assigned them to the tables of the Presidential party and other distinguished guests.

In the literary tradition of the times, the Cambridge girls announced their reasons for offering their services in a formal resolution which was published in the *Sunday Herald* on April 18.

"First, to show our appreciation of, and our devotion to, the cause of liberty, which that day is intended to commemorate; secondly, to exhibit to the world the fact that we glory in being the descendants of the noble women of 1775, who with their own hands did what they could to help forward the

ENTRANCE TO LEXINGTON GREEN

great work of the Revolution, and who considered all honest labor as honorable and praiseworthy."

The City of Boston, having sent a detail of police to Concord, reduced its own protection still further by sending Lieut. Lyman Gould of the 8th Police to Lexington with forty men. They reported for duty on Saturday and were sworn in as town constables by Charles Hudson, Chairman of the Board of Selectmen, at the Lexington town hall. Sergeant Thomas came out with twenty more men on Monday morning.

The selectmen posted a notice around the town forbidding gambling and the sale of liquor during the Centennial and the final period of preparation.

TAKE PARTICULAR NOTICE

As a large collection of people is expected in Lexington on the 19th of April instant, drawn together by our centennial celebration, the selectmen believe that the credit of the town and the comfort and security of the peaceable people who visit the place on that occasion will be promoted by a strict observance of temperance and its kindred virtues. We therefore, the selectmen of said town, hereby forbid the sale of intoxicating liquor in Lexington, and the exhibition or use of cards, dice or other implements of gaming by which money may be gained or lost on the 18th, 19th or 20th of April 1875; and we hereby give notice that we have in all cases of permits prohibited all traffic in ardent spirits and we have engaged a large and efficient force of police and detectives who will be instructed among other things, to allow no liquor traffic nor gambling, but to abate at once every such nuisance as contrary to law and the terms of their permits. The same prohibition will apply to our own citizens and to those who come into town on that occasion.

Charles Hudson	⎧ Selectmen
B. C. Whitcher	⎨ of
Franklin Alderman	⎩ Lexington

As the sun set on Saturday evening the Lexington committee reviewed its preparations and its accomplishments with some satisfaction. All of the public decorations were completed. In the cold and silent dinner tent everything except the food was on the tables. The statues of John Hancock and Samuel Adams, though not in hand, were at least within reach. Lieutenant Gould and his Boston policemen had arrived to enforce the selectmen's admonition on temperance and its kindred virtues. A quiet town went peacefully to sleep.

Sunday morning dawned bleak and cold with a raw wind inspiring the fruitless wish that General Gage had waited another month before sending his troops on their historic mission. Despite the weather large numbers of strangers strolled about the streets admiring the decorations, reading the markers at historic spots and even attending the church services, whose sermons were all devoted to the great occasion.

The crowds in town increased during the day. The Rev. William Adams of New York, formerly of Lexington, came home to open the Centennial Celebration with a grand memorial service in the pavilion tent at seven o'clock Sunday evening. This event had been widely publicized and people came from miles around to hear him. Because of the piercing cold the service was moved to the smaller, but steam-heated, confines of the town hall. All seats were filled long before the appointed hour leaving thousands of disappointed visitors in the street. The committee opened the pavilion tent, therefore, and the Brockton Band generously volunteered to play a concert of music appropriate to the occasion. This they did before a large and appreciative audience. The committee by its resolute action thus met and conquered the first emergency of their Centennial.

All through the night the last pieces were moved into position over the roads. Supply wagons, empty carriages and artillery trains gave way with the dawn to barges, wagons and carriages full of visitors to the celebration. Battery C, First Light Artillery, M. V. M., Lieutenant Boyd commanding, made its way from Boston during the night, took station on Prosser's Hill off Waltham street and greeted the sunrise with a hundred-gun salute.

Traffic on the roads increased steadily in volume. Trains on the Middlesex Central Railroad, their locomotives gaily decked with bunting, steamed into Lexington along their single track from both directions and deposited their passengers into the growing horde. Rail and highway vehicles slowed and finally stopped. The most monumental traffic jam in the history of Massachusetts congealed into a vise-like grip upon the town.

The emotions of the Lexington committee as they watched this tremendous and unexpected response to their Centennial Celebration have not been recorded. Captain Parker and his minute men on Lexington green a hundred years before could not have been any more dismayed when the scarlet coats of the British regulars swung into view.

The Middlesex Central Railroad, a single-track line operated by the Lowell Railroad, provided the only rail service from Boston to Lexington and from Lexington to Concord. Within a few hours it was so blocked up with immense trains that the superintendent of the road telegraphed instructions to Boston to sell no more tickets to Concord. Several thousands of visitors who had unwisely chosen this route to Concord in preference to the double-tracked lines of the Fitchburg Railroad spent the day in Lexington instead.

The Lowell Railroad station in Boston was totally unprepared for the rush. Crowds stormed the ticket windows in unmanageable numbers, careless of the danger to their lives and limbs. An ingenious officer of the railroad escorted ladies to the balcony above the ticket windows, lowered their money on a fish line to the clerks below and pulled up their tickets by the same means.

Fish lines could not be used to pack the ladies on the trains, however, as many ticket holders soon discovered. The young and hardy persisted. The wise gave up the struggle and either sought entertainment in Boston or returned to their homes.

JOHN HANCOCK
BY THOMAS R. GOULD

SAMUEL ADAMS, BY MARTIN MILMORE

The trains were made up in strings of fifteen to thirty cars behind two or three locomotives. Passengers jammed the cars and platforms to the utmost limit. Some even climbed onto the roofs, from which they were driven by the hard-pressed railroad police. The crowd was in a remarkably good temper. The cry, "Room for one more!" emerged in muffled tones from the densely packed cars. For the pickpockets this was indeed a day to remember.

Trains once loaded remained in the station for hours awaiting a clear track ahead. When they finally did move they moved at a snail's pace.

Lexington, reeling under the crowds that poured into her streets, had cause to be grateful that no more people could find transportation.

A cold and piercing wind kept the crowds in motion. Uniformed organizations marched briskly about to the sound of their own music. Pitchmen hawked their wares. The exhibition of Revolutionary relics in the Cary Library drew a capacity crowd desirous of both knowledge and warmth.

The pavilion tent was opened to the public at nine o'clock and quickly filled. The multitude, disappointed, sought entertainment elsewhere. The still air inside the tent seemed even colder than the breeze outside to the audience, who stamped their feet vigorously in an effort to keep warm. They were stamping their feet on a wooden floor laid over a packed snow base, as the workmen discovered on April 20 when the tents were struck. The snow fell on April 13 and still supplied ample refrigeration a week later.

At ten o'clock Thomas Merriam Stetson, President of the Day, opened the ceremonies with a welcome to all. A distinguished New Bedford lawyer, Mr. Stetson was the son of Julia Ann Merriam of Lexington, whose ancestors had been leaders in both Concord and Lexington since the two towns were founded. His career was focused on southern Massachusetts and so lacked the state and federal offices which brought wider recognition to Judge Hoar.

After the customary religious preliminaries, John Greenleaf Whittier recited his poem "Lexington—1775" written especially for the occasion and not written very well, said the *New York Times* on April 18 after reading an advance copy.

"The next act of our ceremonial," said **Mr. Stetson,** "devolves upon one who has done so much for Lexington, her venerable historian, Charles Hudson."

The great audience, sensing the importance of the moment to the speaker, maintained a respectful silence while **Mr. Hudson** sketched swiftly and surely the characters and activities of Samuel Adams and John Hancock as their statues were unveiled.

In retrospect Mr. Hudson's address stands out as the high point in Lexington's Centennial Celebration. It was followed by the main oration of the day. The Honorable Richard Henry Dana, Jr., presented an eloquent, moving and inaccurate account of the battle which thrilled his audience and provided employment to historians for some years thereafter as they pointed out his errors.

A poem by Julia Ward Howe and a benediction pronounced by the Reverend Rollin H. Neale, D.D., concluded the morning program.

"Immediately after these exercises," it is written in the Centennial Proceedings, "the invited guests were escorted to the carriages in waiting, and assigned to their place in the procession, which marched over the designated route, and was reviewed by the President of the United States."

This was the plan and this is a very brief account of what happened. Forming up a procession nearly two miles long in the midst of 100,000 spectators, however, was no easy task. Chief Marshal William A. Tower and his staff accomplished miracles, never once giving way to despair even when President Grant's train from Concord failed to appear.

The column was formed in three divisions on Main street near Bryant's Corner in the eastern part of the town. Some of the marching units arrived too late to take their assigned places in the line. Others, including the Governor of Massachusetts and his escort, did not arrive at all. Once formed, the procession waited more than an hour in the raw and rising east wind under a dusting of snow from passing squalls. Men in formation sang to keep their minds off their discomfort. The less disciplined spectators cursed the delay and the town of Concord which they believed to be responsible for it.

We will now return to President Grant and his party, whom we left outside Concord's oration tent at one o'clock. The railroad station, located between Lowell road and Monument street, was fortunately within easy walking distance of the oration tent. Carriages were provided for the top dignitaries. The others had to walk.

No trains had passed between Concord and Lexington since the early morning rush had clogged the line. The Presidential Special, therefore, was not at the station. There would be no train at the scheduled hour of one o'clock nor could any promise of a train at any time be extracted from the harassed station master.

The Concord committee commandeered enough carriages to start the President, his Cabinet, Governor Chamberlain of South Carolina and a few others over the road to Lexington. Governor Gaston of Massachusetts declined the opportunity to ride with the President, considering it wiser to stay with the members of the Massachusetts legislature, judges and other dignitaries until a train could be had.

The legislators were not in a happy mood. They had marched on foot, four abreast and 200 strong, in the morning procession, much to the astonishment of the spectators, not because they wanted to but because no carriages were provided for them. The blue ribbon each wore with the state coat of arms and a bow of red and white, provided by the Concord and Lexington Centennial Committees, did not console them for their undignified reception.

Two hours later a train reached the Concord station, loaded the chilled and hungry lawmakers, took them to Lexington and deposited them into a far worse tangle than the one they had left. Surely the British regulars a hundred years before had suffered no more than they.

The National Lancers escorted a six-horse carriage to the Munroe Station in East Lexington to await the Presidential Special train. One half hour after the train was due, word reached the Lancers that the President had come by carriage and was stuck in traffic at the other end of town. One hundred and forty-one mounted men, brilliant in their red coats, forced their way through the crowds and rescued the President. Placing him in their grand carriage they escorted him past the entire procession as it stood waiting and took their position with him at the head of the right division. Cheers roaring like surf on a stony beach marked his passage down the line.

Shortly after two o'clock the procession began its march through Main to Hancock street, through Hancock to Revere street, through Revere to Bedford street and thence to the common. The crowd was so dense and the number of stalled teams so numerous that the procession had barely room to pass.

At the end of the route the President of the Day took Mr. Grant, his party and other distinguished guests to his mother's house opposite the common to provide them with much-needed rest and warmth. Then, through two solid ranks of the Ancient and Honorable Artillery Company and the National Lancers, they entered the pavilion tent, paused to admire the statues of Adams and Hancock and continued on to the dinner tent.

There was very little left to admire in the dinner tent. Richmond must have looked like this when it fell to the Federal troops ten years before. Despite the best efforts of the police to stop them, hungry hordes stormed and took the place before it was opened to ticket holders at three o'clock. Once inside the crowd went to work on the food, demolishing caterer Smith's handiwork and reducing the volunteer waitresses from Cambridge to tears. The Arlington volunteers were spared this horrid sight. They had put their

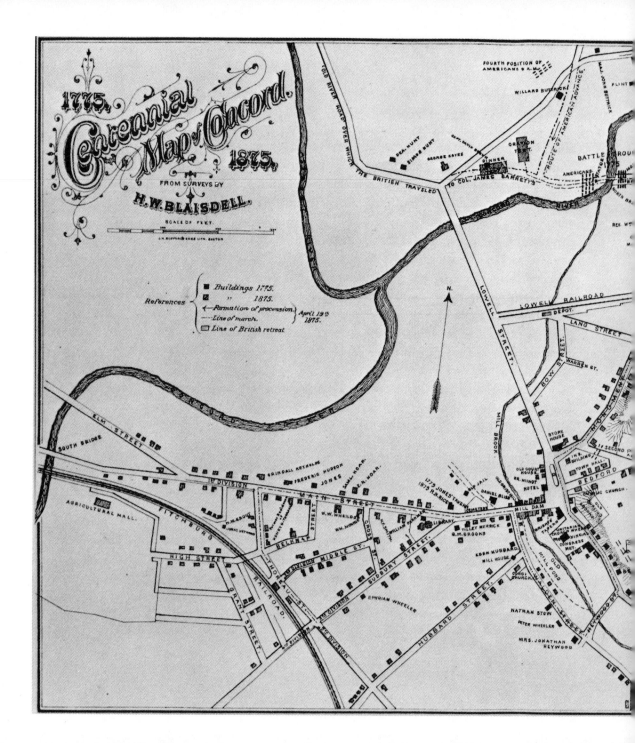

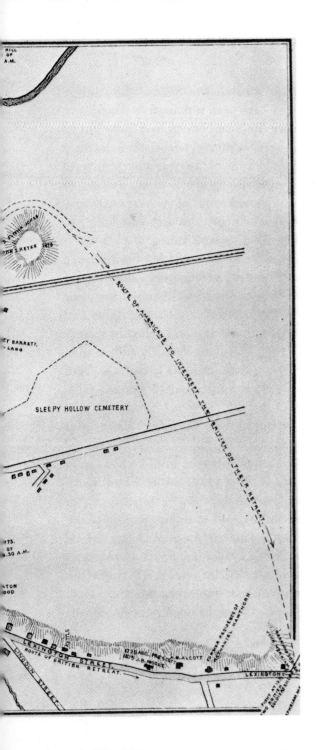

faith in the railroad and never did arrive in Lexington at all.

The ice-cold tent, the tables gutted of their food and the turbulent crowd swarming around the guests of honor combined to diminish the appetites roused by the morning's activities. According to the *Boston Evening Transscript*, "The only thing that was warm at the centennial dinner in Lexington was the ice cream."

The head table was served at about half past three a meal of many courses heralded by an elaborate printed menu whose cover bore an engraving of Jedediah Munroe and whose back page was inscribed "Grand Centennial Banquet, Lexington, 1875." Munroe had been wounded on the common in the morning of April 19, 1775, by Pitcairn's fire, had returned to battle in the afternoon and was killed by Percy's men during their retreat.

Mr. Stetson, President of the Day, looked adversity in the eye with a courage worthy of the steadfast Jedediah. When the dessert appeared on the tables, he requested and received the attention of his vast unruly audience and said:

"Ladies and Gentlemen, the lapse of a century of national life, during which the pageant and insignia of royalty have been unknown to Americans, has brought us together at the spot where American liberty first spoke out its purpose and determination. The nation bends with reverence before the plain gravestone, with its inscription that reads like one of the tablets of eternity, of the first Martyrs of the Revolution. Their battle, with its calm courage, its personal heroism, its strange, bold, unexpected stand of sixty against eight hundred, was the flower and consummation of principles that were long ripening in the clear-sighted, liberty-loving, Anglo-Saxon mind."

In the course of his short, incisive address he reminded his audience that Lexington had instructed its representative as to his course concerning the obnoxious acts of Parliament, "so to vote, that, whether successful or not, succeeding generations may know that we understood our rights and liberties, and were neither ashamed nor afraid to assert and maintain them."

Substituting the word "act" for "vote," Captain Parker's minute men defended this policy to the death a few years later. A study of the records of this Centennial shows that Mr. Stetson and his committee acted on the same high standard.

Mr. Stetson ended his remarks by introducing President Grant, who rose to his feet and was greeted with tremendous applause.

As the Governor of Massachusetts was still engaged in the retreat from Concord, Mr. Stetson called on Governor Daniel H. Chamberlain of South Carolina to reply to a toast to his state.

South Carolina was the first colony to respond to the suggestion of the Massachusetts legislature in June of 1764 that an American congress be formed of delegates from each of the thirteen colonies. South Carolina in 1875 was doing her best to heal the wounds left by the War Between the States. The palmetto tree in the oration tent bore witness to this and so did the palmetto leaves shipped to Lexington by Colonel Courtney of the Washington Light Infantry of Charleston which were worn in the hats, button-holes and muskets of the Ancient and Honorable Artillery Company during the procession.

Mr. Chamberlain ended his speech with a plea for a monument to be erected in the hearts of all the American people, the monument of a reunited country, a free and just government, an indestructible Union of indestructible States.

What the States needed most on this occasion was indestructible officers. As Mr. Chamberlain spoke the Governor of Massachusetts, the Chief Justice of the Supreme Judicial Court, other judges and the General Court of Massachusetts staggered into the tent, cold, dinnerless and exhausted. The Governor had succeeded in turning the retreat into a personal triumph, however. He had stayed with his legislators throughout their most harrowing corporate experience, thus earning their forgiveness for his political error of riding in a carriage during the morning procession when they were forced to walk.

"I regret that I was not here to respond to this toast when it was first called," said Governor Gaston in reply to "The Commonwealth of Massachusetts" from the chair. "I did my best to get here, and have been working three hours before I could succeed."

Following his brief speech of welcome to the distinguished guests, in his capacity as Governor of Massachusetts, he yielded the floor again to Mr. Stetson, who read the message from Concord carried by President Grant. The audience received it with deafening applause and cheers.

President Grant, his mission accomplished, left the tent quietly with Chief Marshal Tower and went to the Tower home for a rest. The 4th Battalion, M. V. M., called on him there, hoping for the honor of a presidential inspection. The President obliged, much to the pleasure of the soldiers, and returned to his fireside.

Other distinguished guests soon followed the President's example and slipped away in search of warmth or transportation away from the Centennial area. Voices outside the tent were clearly audible inside as the cold, curious or merely drunk argued with the police in an effort to enter.

Now was the time for two old campaigners to depart from the script long long enough to revive flagging spirits. Mr. Stetson toasted the Orator of the Day. Their remarks, which were published without comment in the Proceedings, take on an entirely different meaning in the light of the newspaper accounts of the day.

"Do you not think Mr. Dana owes us two speeches today?" Mr. Stetson asked. "I am about to propose a toast to entice him from his ease and comfort at this table; and, if he will speak to us again, we will hold that he has earned the right to silence till—our next Centennial."

Mr. Dana rose nobly to the bait.

"I understood you to say, sir, that you mean to entice me from my ease and comfort. Now, I should like to know what description of ease and comfort will describe the situation we have been in the last half-hour. An official, duly decked out with a ribbon, passed this way, and told us, 'The speeches are to be omitted; and wisely,' he added, looking hard at some of us. So we felt safe; when I saw all eyes turned upon me, and caught a few of your last words. I understood you to say that I owed one more speech to the people on this occasion. Well, sir, I admit the debt, but I intend to go into bankruptcy. . . . Now, you are all so comfortably situated, you have all had so much to eat and so much to drink, and you have all found it so easy to get here, and you will all find it so easy to get back again, that I am very sure you are in the best possible spirits, and that all you wish is for the speaking to go on, and to hear as many speakers as you possibly can. I understand that the judges of the supreme court, who have been traveling all day, have got somewhere at last; they have arrived at this place dinnerless, and without any written opinion in their pockets; but the Chief Justice will be called upon to pronounce his opinion of all that has occurred to him and the rest of us today. . . . Lexington used to give very warm receptions to her enemies. They did a hundred years ago. I suppose you thought you ought not to treat your friends in the same way. We will never complain of it, on that score. Mr. President, I will not take the time that I know so many gentlemen about me are desirous to occupy, anxious to be unexpectedly called upon; and so I will return to you my thanks, and take my seat."

The Honorable Horace Gray, Chief Justice of Massachusetts, replied to the toast "The Bench and Bar" with a prepared address containing a judicial opinion upon the state of affairs on the morning of the battle of Lexington. He wisely omitted any mention of a judicial opinion on the hardships he had so far survived on the anniversary.

Toast followed toast in the freezing tent. Some were present to respond to them. Others had already fled. Some replied briefly and extended their remarks in the Proceedings. The hour of adjournment is not recorded.

Outside the tents morning enthusiasm slacked off to evening distress. Long before noon many of the visitors attempted to leave town only to discover that the means for doing so decreased even faster than their desire to escape increased. One train left for Boston at ten o'clock, packed with passengers inside and out. It arrived at noon. All day long the railroad station was surrounded by a densely packed mass of people, tired, cold, hungry and anxious to depart. A reporter for the *Boston Daily Globe* estimated a total of 4,000 passengers in and on the twenty-nine cars of a train which left for Boston at a quarter past four. Two locomotives were barely able to move it.

Crowds walked the railroad tracks out of town hoping to intercept a train. Others walked the roads back to civilization where horse-cars and the Fitchburg Railroad were able to speed them on their way. Bonfires of rail fences lighted the route and warmed the retreating celebrants.

The Dedham delegation suffered as much as any. After the ceremonies

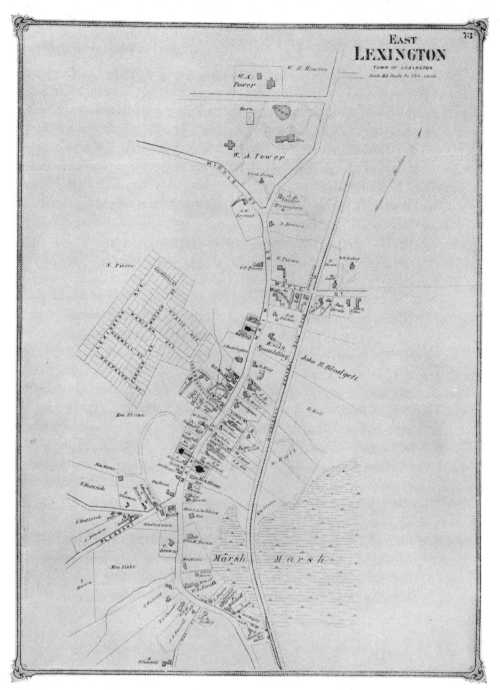

MAP OF EAST LEXINGTON, 1875

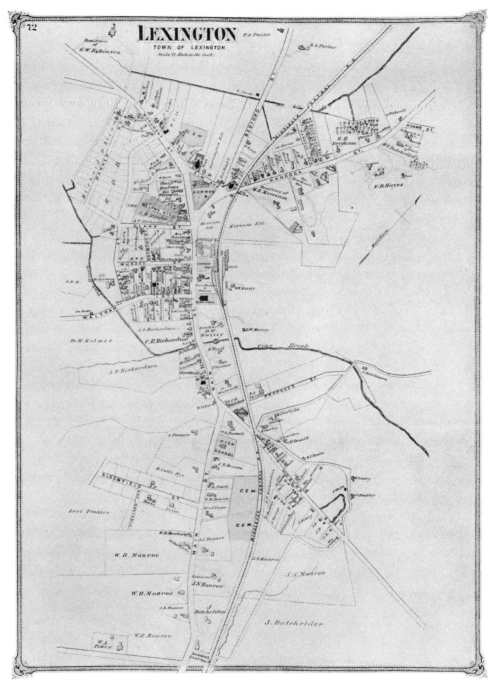

MAP OF LEXINGTON, 1875

in the tent, their marshal, General Thomas Sherwin, led his group of 150 citizens, 40 veterans from the G. A. R. Post No. 144 and the Dedham Brass Band to a bleak hilltop on the edge of town. Here they waited nearly two hours, huddled around a bonfire, while their leaders pondered a means of escape. They then marched to Waltham, suffering two casualties on the way from the hit-and-run tactics of a "Boston dragoon." At the Waltham railroad station a third man was hurt in a fall. Most of the group arrived home by midnight, having had a harder time during the retreat from Lexington than their ancestors did.

Mayor Williams, the City Government of Salem, the Salem Band and 109 Salem Cadets had better luck. They walked to Arlington and took the horse-cars to Boston and the railroad home.

Earl Percy's cannon could not have cleared the road today.

The *Boston Daily News* summed up the situation in a paragraph published on Wednesday, April 21. "There is no difficulty *now* in understanding the early and hurried retreat of the British from Concord and Lexington to Boston. They were level headed."

Alcohol added to the problems of those obliged to enjoy the Centennial to the bitter end. The Selectmen's wise prohibition of all traffic in ardent spirits was ignored, even by Lexington's one hotel. Food was scarce but liquor flowed in abundance and minor brawls abounded.

The police tried to reduce the supply of strong drink but with limited success. There were, after all, only sixty police in town. Five hundred would have had their hands full.

The first liquor seizure of the day was made by Officer Morse of the Third Police precinct of Boston. James Murphy was the unfortunate victim. When he was arrested his wagon was found to contain assorted liquors amounting to four dozen half-pint bottles, two dozen pint bottles, and a gallon jug. Business was so brisk that, had Officer Morse delayed his arrival another ten minutes, James Murphy's wagon would have been bare and Jimsie as innocent of wrongdoing as a newborn lamb. Other salesmen were more fortunate.

The northeast wind went down with the sun and the temperature dropped to the low twenties. The cold air numbed the hungry, helpless crowds beyond the powers of alcohol to remedy. The inhabitants of Lexington, looking out from their warm houses, were moved to compassion, opened their doors to the strangers in the streets and fed them to the limits of their larders. Churches, too, offered shelter, filling their pews and aisles with overnight guests.

Despite the cold the grand levee and ball in the large pavilion drew an estimated 2,000 persons. President Grant and his cabinet arrived shortly after nine as Brown's Brigade Band and the Germania orchestra were playing a promenade concert. Those who wished to shake the President by the hand had an ample opportunity to do so.

After an hour of this the President and his party, the Governor of South Carolina, the Chief Marshal, the President of the Day and several members of the Centennial Committee left the pavilion and returned to the main entrance of the common. Here, by request of the citizens of Lexington, the President planted a young elm tree. The streets were now empty. The full moon shone down through the cold, still air. All was quiet except for the sound of music from the tent. Thinking back on his hectic day, President Grant declared that no feature of the exercises of the day had given him more pleasure than this last one.

The group then entered a nearby house to warm themselves once more. At about half past ten they took carriages for Boston. The original plan had called for the President to return to the ball in Concord. There are limits, however, to human endurance.

The ladies of Lexington knew no such limits. They came to the ball in their best evening dresses with low necks and short sleeves and danced happily till the dawn. Their escorts wore overcoats, cloaks and mufflers to ward off the cold, causing people to wonder if women are indeed the weaker sex.

On Tuesday morning, April 20, Lexington began to take on again its customary appearance. Railroad trains ran on schedule, full but not jammed with departing guests. Many of the cars bore the scars of the Centennial. Scraped paint, leaky roofs, smashed seats, doors and windows were mute reminders of the chaos now passed.

The tents on the common were struck and hauled away at an early hour. Willing hands moved the statues of Hancock and Adams to their niches in Memorial Hall to stand in company with those of the minute man and the soldier of 1861. Of all the additions to the skyline of the common only the slender aspiring branches of a small elm tree remained to mark the events of the previous day.

In the words of the Centennial Proceedings, "May this little tree, planted on this memorable occasion, strike deep its roots, and throw out its branches under the fostering care of the people of Lexington; so that when the next centennial shall bring other multitudes to the old shrine of liberty, they may pause under its shade, and rejoice with patriotic pride, that, during the growth of this memorial tree, the country has made equal progress in all the elements that constitute a nation's greatness!"